LIVING IN THE FLOW

Demystifying Manifesting & Co-creating a Life of Ease

BY

BERNICE ANGOH

Cover Design: Bernice Angoh

Printed in the United States of America

Special Thank You to Cathy Sares

First Printing, 2021
ISBN: 978-1-7355053-6-7
Publisher: www.paperheartbook.com

TABLE OF CONTENTS

INTRODUCTION

In this book we will be exploring the phenomenon called "Manifesting," to demystify what it is through a handful of my own personal stories of "manifesting." These personal accounts are a minor illustration of my journey to effortless creating and living a life of ease and flow; to show you the different circumstances I went through to find a simple truth. I hope you enjoy it, but more so, I hope you get a glimpse into the life that is already yours: To know that your participation is all but inspired--a thing needing little or no effort on your part. So, relax into the dream.

There is nothing left to do,
little dreamer!

PRAISE

"The simplicity with which Bernice presents spiritual matters strikes a chord within the heart of every demographic, confirming the knowledge we all are connected and share similar issues. In the simplest of ways, she taught me how to let go, not just let go, but let go with love. That way, you get love right back in its purest form. I used to take what she told me with a pinch of salt until I started to see how the universe unraveled itself before my eyes very quickly confirming it's not rocket science and it's accessible to all with an open mind. She made me understand the magic to all of this is 'love'. Her message on love and forgiving gave me the transformation I desperately needed and has now become a constant in my daily life. Our conversations felt like she was reading my mind and "Yes!", "Yes!", "Yes!" almost became my mantra. One of the deepest truths I learned from Bernice that has stuck with me is "What you see reflects you" which accentuated the power of thought and visualization."

- Elizabeth Beseka, USA

"Bernice is a magical and inspirational being. Her devotion to elevating others through presence of beauty compels each of us to answer the divine call within."

- Alessandra Rossi-Filippi, Germany

"The compassionate motherly love that I always get from you and the way you listen, lending your caring heart, mind and body and giving your all for the welfare of all involved is incomparable and is such a blessing as more than half the healing is done there and there as I see it and experienced it too.

The noble work you are doing here now if I must sum up, I fumble to find the right adjective and the correct words for it as it's beyond words and I am speechless ...

All I can say is that you're just like a mother to the world; sharing and caring, giving all your love unconditionally for the greatest good of all involved.

Sending you loads and loads of love, light, and blessings. Carry on and keep spreading the divine light of love and compassion, the world needs more such angels like you here now."
-Priyajit Das, India

"I've had the privilege to have Bernice as my mentor, spiritual coach and a really good friend. I always turn to her for advice/help when feel under-stress or if something is bothering me inside and she always helps me out with her lovely words and wonderful advice, which to me has always been helpful and gets me out of that stressful state almost immediately at most times and after a small while, other times. She is very approachable and always understands the core of my problems so she can give me the best advice. I would highly recommend Bernice as a spiritual coach."
-Zarar Ali, U.K

Bernice writes with unflinching soul stirring passion and incisive poetic harmony, harnessing humanistic perspectives - weaving and interlinking our common human impulses and experiences in relatable and easy to digest prose. As we reflect, we are irredeemably inspired and refreshed.
-Nna Emeka, USA

A pure playful light being, in her presence I felt like I am with a Divine Angel feeling Safe and magnificently softly loved and cared for and her words of deep wisdom, light , laughter and infinite possibilities of creation on this earth are incredible. Her words of love touch deep into my heart and soul, my heart flowers with beauty with her love and words expressed so gracefully and eloquently her words are like a wand of wonder and magic that are deeply touching and profoundly inspiring, when I read her Poetry or speak to her she invokes my own love to expand and create a world of abundant beauty that I want to live in. So much love and appreciation Bernice xx Gorgeous, Graceful, Alchemist writing!

-Nancy Joyce Hunter. UK

"You are a beautiful blessing to this world. I am grateful to you from the core of my heart for being an amazing, wonderful source of inspiration and motivation. With your company, I have become increasingly positive, confident, and strong. I feel blessed that I met you and life changed lovingly. Your prayers and blessings for my friends even worked successfully. Thank you, Bernice, for everything."

-Suchi Arora, India

"When you come to Bernice Angoh with any life complications, she is skilled and ready to advise you on just the right common-sense advice. Thank you, Bernice for your great messages of love for ourselves and others. Most of all, thank you for being a prime example of all the beautiful teachings you bless us with! Thank you for the love and blessings that you have poured into my life. My sister Bernice, you are truly MAGICAL! Whenever I read anything from you, I leave this world of Caesar for a moment and just become one through your beautiful writings! Continue to create Magic through your beautiful writings, morning, noon, and night because you are changing the world every word at a time! Peace and Love"

-Yvrose Mshihiri, USA

I was drawn to Bernice from her Facebook writings. Something about what she writes speaks purity to me. Her writing gives rhythm to silence and light to darkness. Very therapeutic and helps me understand the significance of words themselves. It gives me insights of myself that I never knew existed but always wanted to know. Her writing gives me the power to self-worth and complete understanding of my identity, slows the world down around me and streamlines thoughts to short direct sentences while soothing the anxiety out of my body with a lyrical style. It makes me think and practice Love.

-Evangeline Mecaly, UK

Bernice Angoh is a fountain of wisdom. She is inspiration personified. The poignant simplicity of her work keeps the reader captivated right to the very last word. The way she expresses life and above all LOVE is magical. Reading her work always leaves me wondering how many thousands of lives she has lived before this one and knowing how young she is, it's just mind-blowing. She is a beautiful person and it's a unique privilege to know her.

-Jayne Taku, USA

Creation is an unsuspecting process, a barely perceivable, on-going process of clearing the mind from cobwebs of distractions piled on by society, belief, and conditioning. Creation occurs when we get out of our own way.

~BERNICE ANGOH

Ricky-Kinda-Guy

I love to tell this story because it happened when I didn't know much about the term "Manifesting." I was about sixteen, and all I had was my amazing imagination and a powerful desire to have the things I imagined.

As a young girl growing up in Cameroon, West Africa, reading was my favorite form of entertainment. As an avid reader, I especially enjoyed reading romance novels when I could. Reading served as a beautiful escape for me. I loved to speak my intentions aloud, so often, and to whomever would listen. It brought me joy to 'fantasize'. I didn't know back then I was painting what would become my reality, even though inside I hoped for it to be so. Make-believe was one of my favorite pastimes.

Fast-forward several years later, I am twenty four, married, with a beautiful baby girl, and living in America. One day, the phone rings and it was my aunt. She was screaming on the other side of the phone. The first thing that came to my mind was that something bad had happened to my mom, but thankfully she calmed my fears.

"You need to sit down for this!"

"Okay, I am." I lied. I was too nervous to sit.

"Okay, you're going to flip out!"

"My goodness, Aunty, tell me already!" I was getting frustrated.

"Okay, so you remember when you were younger and used to drive us crazy with all this your wild imaginations and dreams?"

With a sigh of relief, I said, "Yes."

"Remember when you said you will get married at 23 and have your first child at 24?"

"Yes." I whispered. I had forgotten all about it.

"Do you remember talking about the man you will marry? And what did you used to say about him?" She asked.

At this point my hands were shaking. "I said he would be a Ricky-kinda' guy." ("Ricky-kinda' guy" was our code word for "cute" --There was this cute Italian guy named Ricky on a novella we used to watch.)

But here's the kicker, my husband's name was Ricky, and he was part Italian! We got married under unusual circumstances when I was twenty-three and had our first child when I was twenty-four! (Interesting enough there were two miscarriages before but somehow the words I spoke 'nailed' me to that promise of having that baby, and the universe held on to that age, 24)

We were both screaming on the phone when she said, "All your dreams have come true. Everything you said has happened!"

It sent chills down my body, and it was with that realization that I went to fulfill another dream of mine to become a published author.

It is true, imagination is KEY, and the doorway is FEELING it passionately enough to do your part(act) when inspired to. Your dreams are just waiting for you to arrive so they can say to you, "Hello there! I've been waiting for you ever since you first conjured me up!"

You are always the participant-observer, simultaneously, and sometimes unconsciously, making waves and creating worlds as you go.

~BERNICE ANGOH

FEAR IS A GUIDE

GO CONFIDENTLY TOWARDS IT. (LEMONADE STREET)

I was a stay-at-home mom who also homeschooled her daughter. Although I enjoyed every moment of my role as a stay-at-home mom, my dream of becoming a published author always nagged me. I started writing at an early age, ten to be exact--it was a way to cope after my molestation. By the time I was fifteen I had several hundred songs, countless poems, and a dozen short stories. I had been in America for a little while and with each year I saw my dreams go farther and farther from reach. I kept writing none the less.

To contribute to household finances, I took a job as a waiter at IHOP. Being an introvert and loving my solitude, I was shy and didn't like to be around people for extended periods of time. I wasn't sure how I would be able to walk up to strangers and strike a conversation while I served them. But I needed the job badly. The hours were convenient for my daughter's homeschooling schedule. I worked Friday to Sunday nights at IHOP, and during the week I was my daughter's teacher. It was hectic but I had no choice. Plus, I really did want to build the right learning foundation for my child; the only reason I homeschooled instead of getting a full-time job.

Despite my fear, I accepted the position to work at IHOP. It was one of the most rewarding jobs I've ever had. I learned so many important and useful skills that I would later use in life as a speaker and a coach. Working at IHOP made me a much better communicator and a less shy person. Most importantly, the job that I was most scared to do ended up being the doorway for publishing my first book. I met Aerle, one of the members of the prominent 80s R&B groups "Arrested Development", at IHOP. As I waited on her, we began talking about poetry and literature. It was she who introduced me to the publisher. The rest as they say is history.

Had I turned down the job out of fear; had I let fear paralyze me into submission; had I said no when offered the position; had I not had the courage to look past my biggest fear, I wouldn't have published my first poetry book, *Lemonade Street.*

Fear is a guide, walk confidently with her.

From the immaculate conception of your thoughts, your "babies" arise from the womb of your heart.

~BERNICE ANGOH

A BABY STORY

If you take the time to look at your life, you will see how you co-created almost everything. Ever since I was a child, I've had an unquenchable passion and stubbornness to have the things I love and desire. It has helped me so much, even though it has not always been 'rosy'.

I discovered for the first time that I co-created my life when I was 24 (previously mentioned). The confidence I gained from that helped me to assist others in co-creating their dreams. This baby story I'm about to share was such fun. I told this story to someone else who reached out to me privately for encouragement during a challenging time in her marriage and she also got favorable results.

I had just moved to a new city as a newly separated mom with two children. Before I found work at the children's hospital, I braided clients' hair-- a skill that saved me when times were hard.

My clients always felt safe sharing with me. It has always been that way since I was in high school. People felt comfortable telling me their deepest, darkest secrets and I listened, comforted, and advised as best as I knew how. At one point I contemplated becoming a counselor, but later settled for being just a listening ear—I didn't want to spend those years in school trying to get a degree.

Anyway, back to the story. This client wanted to have children, but the doctors had told her she couldn't. They didn't give her any precise reason. She was frustrated and worried because she was in her forties and her ovaries were not getting any younger (her words).

I asked her what she truly desired and she said she really wanted to give herself and her husband a baby; I suppose there was also stress coming from relatives and in-laws.

I said to her, "Well then, you'll have your baby! Just don't give up." I started doing her hair in 2013. Every time she came back to redo her hair, she gave me updates. I sent her information on natural aids for cleansing the entire body, as I had done with a friend who later bore a child after six years of trying everything under the sun.

My client told me in 2014 she'd gotten pregnant but later miscarried. All attempts using IVF (In-vitro fertilization) had failed as well. I said, "Well, doesn't mean a thing, you want this baby?" She answered, "That's all I ever wanted, and I will do anything to have a baby." I sent her some words of encouragement and told her to not give up.

When next I saw her, she was completely worn out and almost giving up. She had had at least four miscarriages so far. I chose not to pity her but tell her some inspiring stories.

"You're too anxious and too tensed. Relax, go out and buy baby stuff. Start decorating your nursery" I said. To which she reluctantly agreed. In my heart I thought, *my goodness, I only have to kiss a man and I'll be pregnant. But look at this wonderful woman, all she wants is one child!*

I saw her again in mid-2015. She said she'd been more relaxed, and that she and her husband have been going out and not thinking too much about having a baby. She then turned to me and said, "Maybe I wasn't meant to have a baby, my husband wouldn't mind, he loves me a lot!" I realized she was trying to console herself. She was giving up.

I replied, "Girlfriend! When you have this baby, it won't even be one! It will be twins even, and who knows, it'd be a boy and a girl then you'd be done. You'd have one of each in one go, boom!" We both burst out laughing.

She said, "Well, I guess I can try again."

I said, "Heck yeah, do it."

During the time she was away we communicated briefly. Whenever I could, I imagined lovingly for her. I imagined her telling me she was pregnant.

She called me a few months later to tell me she was pregnant, and that this time she had gone longer into the pregnancy than previous times. When she came by to braid her hair, she voiced her fears.

"What if ..."

I stopped her from finishing her sentence, encouraged her not to let doubt creep in, and told her to keep shopping for baby clothes and continue decorating the nursery. I sent her guided meditations, affirmations, and mantras to speak and some to listen to when, and if, she got anxious.

The next time she came to do hair she announced, "Guess what! It's twins!"

You can imagine how loud I was screaming, and then she finished with, "It's a boy and a girl!"

Boy, oh boy!

I mean, come on!

We were hysterical, gleaming from ear to ear.

After the great moment of jubilation, she said, "You've been with me through this, and I'd love for you to be my doula!" She wanted me to assist her in the labor room during delivery. I was very honored, and even though I didn't get to fulfill her wish due to certain constraints, it was a sweet thought.

The day I finally visited her to see those twin babies, I thought, *My goodness! The power of belief and persistence!* Miscarriages can be very discouraging, but she never gave up. At the time I was writing this book, the twins were six months old.

Anything is possible! You just must be crazy enough to believe the impossible... you're already crazy in other areas in life, employ that craziness for what you desire. If you have friends or know anyone who truly desires something good in their lives, the best you can do is lend them your crazy and your obnoxious belief that they could have what they desire by giving them words of encouragement and a little imagination.

Be foolish for your dreams, be crazy, be stupid. No one must believe you. You have enough belief for yourself even if it's just the craziest idea you've ever had.

When you look back in your life at the major things that happened, you will be able to trace most of it back to a thought or something you said. Your word goes forward to build a bridge between the material and immaterial world, especially if what you desire is strongly felt.

I hope all your desires come easily and swiftly! And congratulations to all the mothers to-be; your babies are beautiful! (wink, wink) Keep believing them into being.

Jesus Christ knew he was God. So, wake up and find out eventually who you really are. In our culture, of course, they will say you are crazy, and you are blasphemous, and they will either put you in jail or in a nut house (which is pretty much the same thing). However, if you wake up in India and tell your friends and relations, 'My goodness, I've just discovered that I'm God,' they will laugh and say, 'Oh, congratulations, at last you found out.

~ALAN WATTS

LITTLE CREATORS

(GOD IN YOU)

Let me share this funny story about how bold and smart children are. Well, my son came back from church one day, he was five then. He looked at me and said, "Mama why do people say god is good when he's not?"

So, I asked "Why do you say that?" He said because they were teaching them the story of Noah and the ark, and he doesn't understand why God would kill people, even children and animals. He was appalled. I was happy he asked that question because there was a struggle between me and his dad--and the in laws; they worried that I would push my views on the kids since at that point I had left organized religion all together. I didn't understand why I should burden their impressionable minds with something that was not given the esoteric interpretation it deserved.

So yes, I was so pleased that this little boy on his own would ask questions that adults were scared to ask for fear of being thrown into hell. I took this opportunity to explain to him that bible stories were mostly fables, metaphors, and allegories. He quickly understood because it finally made more sense to him--otherwise it was madness to call someone who kills children and animals a good person.

Anyway, a friend of mine came by once and my son, Ricky, decided to ask her, "Do you believe in God?" She responded, " Of course I do!"

I held my breath because I could see where this was going. This friend of mine was a Christian. Ricky further explained, "Well, I do believe in God but not like you do. I believe that I Am god and mommy is god and you are god, and god is in everything!" Apparently my son had been going around telling all his little friends that he is god and they are god too! When I heard this I cringed because we lived in an area with very religious folks, so I had to have a conversation with him about how to deal with this his wonderful confidence--which I terribly enjoyed and encouraged-- while respecting other people's beliefs. He then asked me, "So mama when I'm in school and they are praying, what should I do?" I said, "You don't have to say what they say if you don't feel comfortable doing it!" He got excited and replied, "I know what I'll do mama! I'll just close my eyes and meditate, and while they are praying, I will quietly recite 'OM MANI PADME HUM!"

I'd rather let my children wonder in awe of the universe and then come to whatever conclusions that give them peace. I expose them to different schools of thought, and other esoteric religious interpretations of texts. That gives them the choice to be pulled intuitively where their soul's path will lead.

At night when he asks me to make up a bedtime story--I tell him stories about his wonderful imagination. Every character in the stories I make up illustrates how they co-create their realities from thought conception, the balancing act of persistence and letting go, and most importantly inspired action. I figured it was a wonderful way to start planting these seeds into the minds of our not-so-little creators!

Sat-Chit-Ananda♥

When you imagine, you're seeing into what already is or was. Everything you can imagine-- and every desire-- is either a memory or a premonition.

~BERNICE ANGOH

DON'T WORRY ABOUT TOMORROW

Think on that statement and contemplate its implication: When you are too preoccupied with the future, you're missing the most integral part of that same future which is NOW, the present, being here and now. When you look at yourself as lesser and put whatever is your desire on a pedestal, then you've simply switched positions with the object of your desire. Now that thing or person on the pedestal governs over you. You cannot worship the creation, yet we do it over and over... for example, those trying to manifest a specific person: Sometimes this person becomes so important that we make ourselves so small in our own eyes, or completely forget to put ourselves first. We become lost in them and totally lose our sense of self in the process ... In many ways we beg for their love! I mean darn it! Why are they--or should they be-- more precious than you? Why don't you elevate yourself and say, "I'm phenomenal? And this should be reciprocal. They should hold me in high esteem the same way I hold them in high esteem."

It's a proccss, and until you come to that place of utter confidence in self and total love of self, nothing will change in your outer world... why? Because we project what we hold inside. We must stop the begging and the desperation, for it's very counter intuitive to what we are wanting to manifest--who doesn't like a confident person? I've learned that love, unconditional love, is non-attachment, it lives without expectation... plus the love you desire only comes from Source....you, and only you, generate that very love which you desire in your beloved ...you will only be given what you already have. It is a mirroring effect.

THE MIRRORING EFFECT

When you stand in front of a mirror, you don't expect your reflection to smile first before you smile. No, you smile first, and then it is reflected to you from the mirror. Simply, you must become the state into which you want to enter. If you want to have a life partner, act, and feel as if you already have one. You must align with the frequency of being loved and cared for. You should remain content and thankful.

I remember reaching a point when I didn't even care if my ex returned or not... I even looked at myself once and said, "You even deserve better than this man you're fighting for. Look at you, see how magnificent you are!" I mean, I was totally in love with me. I was ALL that, and I finally recognized it. (I tell this story later in the book)

I love when my Higher-Self reminds me, "Bernice, why even fuss? Haven't I always brought you to the right place at the right time and to the right people at the perfect time?" Made me remember the verse in the Bible that says ... look at the flowers in the field and the birds they don't worry about what to eat, they are clothed and fed. (paraphrasing big time here!)

The only benefit of being awake is to GET OUT OF YOUR OWN WAY...

Live life in the NOW, shift your focus towards helping others ... enjoy life and CAST YOUR BURDENS upon I AM (Source, The Divine, God, The Great Spirit) and leave the rest to the universe to connect all the supposedly synchronized, random events that will bring you to yourself.

*If having a **soul** means being able to feel love, loyalty, and gratitude, then **animals** are better off than a lot of humans.*

~JAMES HERRIOT

MUST LOVE DOGS
(EVEN DOGS FALL IN LOVE)

So, every time I go out to the back of the house to exercise or meditate, my friend's dog, Wesley, comes with me... he usually entertains himself while I exercise. Once I'm done exercising, I go towards the trees to meditate and absorb some glorious sunlight. During that time, Wesley usually stays by my side or plays with the neighbor's dog from across the fence.

Many times I've thought, oh wouldn't it be nice if they were on the same side of the fence playing together and in contact/touching each other.

Well, one day it happened! I thought, *omg how did it happen? The other dog is so little he couldn't possibly have jumped over that fence to come to Wesley.*

Apparently, the little dog and Wesley had both been digging underneath the fence from their corresponding sides. The hole was big enough for the little dog to get under the fence and into my friend's yard.

That morning I was able to 'catch' them again in the act of a 'secret rendezvous' (yup, that's the writer and romantic in me)

I even saw them nose-kiss! I melted .... I love it!

Wesley and the neighbor's dog.

p.s Unfortunately the neighbor discovered the little hole they dug underneath the fence and closed it off.

The very act of not letting go or surrendering is missing the mark: for I tell you, your ways and thoughts are unmatched to what the universe can cook up and serve you. Don't worry about the how, just put your intention out and follow with action. Let go and let GOOD in!

~BERNICE ANGOH

DESPARATION/ ANXIETY

Desperation will bring you nothing but frustration
Frustration will give you nothing but condemnation
Condemnation will bring you nothing but damnation
--You damn the other, you damn yourself--
Damnation will bring you nothing but entrapment
Entrapment is a self-prescribed coffin
My friend, why would you ever opt to be the walking dead?

Dreams were not meant to enslave us; they are meant to liberate us: let go! Holding on means you lack trust/knowingness. Flow with what comes and change with the changing tides of life, it is a dance anyway, so let yourself be gently led.

~BERNICE ANGOH

YOU ARE ALWAYS DRAWING UNTO YOU THOSE THINGS YOU RELAX ABOUT

A few days ago, my friend and I were watching a Keanu Reeves movie titled "Knock-knock," and I thought *hmm, I must get her to watch 'Hard Candy' starring one of my favorite actors, Ellen Page.* It was just a one-second thought. I never told my friend about it.

The next day, she asks me to come ride with her to the library because she needed somethings printed. When we get there, she says to me, "See if there are any good movies." Well, I go to the movie section and the very first thing I see right in front of me is the movie 'Hard Candy." Coincidence? I think not!

Before we left the house for the library, I had said to her, "You love romantic movies a lot and I'm telling you, you have to watch a Bollywood movie with me, and I know just the one!" In my mind I thought I'd get her to watch 'Jab tak hai jaan' starring the amazing Shah Rukh Khan.

So, back to the library scene: I'm standing there with the 'Hard Candy' movie in my hand, and I decided to look at the shelf directly below and there it was...you guessed right! 'Jab tak hai jaan'

This is how the universe works. It's like going to the library and asking the clerk for a particular book which he searches in the computer, goes down an aisle and gets it for you. Sometimes the clerk says, "I'll put it on hold and call you when we get it in this location." Sometimes we get what we want instantly and sometimes we must hold on for it to get 'here', but only if we don't get attached to the outcome, only if we let go of the thought.

When you know it's there you don't fret or panic or wonder...you're just excited!

Waiting is resisting; it is much different from patience. Waiting has an anxiety attached to it. The moment you start to wait is the moment you start to resist. When you resist the moment, the moment resists you; it doesn't let you be. So, just be, so that what must happen will flow to you without restriction.

- MARC LEE

PRACTICE WITH FUN

STORY 1--TOM

I was talking to my friend, Hina, about how I've been having premonitions: I see and hear things before they happen... they announce themselves to me first and then I experience it in the physical.

One day, I had the urge to write to my friend Tom, but then I thought I'll just summon him to write me, to reach out to me.

Later that afternoon, I said to Hina watch and see, he will write me and tell me Merry Christmas!

About an hour or so later, I'm checking my email and I have a message from Tom (Not the Tom who's my friend.) but what was fascinating was the message this other Tom wrote!

The message was from a contact on LinkedIn. Didn't know him and had never communicated with him before. He wrote, "Hi Bernice, how are you? I just wanted to wish you Merry Christmas!" This person had been part of my network but never reached out to me before then.

STORY 2- THE ROSE

The next thing I did was imagine a red rose. I said "Higher-Self, I'd like to see a rose or see someone get a rose." The very next day, a friend asked if I wanted to go to the movies with her. I really didn't want to go, but I had turndown so many of her invites before, so, I said, yes.

I asked her what movie we were going to watch, and she replied, "Fences" with Denzel Washington and Viola Davis. We got to the movie theatre and started watching the movie. Way into the middle of the movie, Denzel's brother, brings a rose to his brother's wife and says, "Here is a rose for you Rose." I almost fell off my chair. And he didn't just offer her a rose once, he offered it repeatedly. I thought that was cool.

DREAMS

Dreams>Drames

At one point, while learning how the conscious and subconscious mind operate, I began experiencing different things in my dreams. For some time, I would dream and if it wasn't going well, I'd be aware it's just a dream and allow myself to experience it knowing I'd wake up eventually.

If something happened that I didn't like, I would stop and say, "Nope that's not how I want it." And then I'd change it, or I'll simply deny its implication in my dream. I've stopped someone from trying to get in my dream and be intimate with me before. I remember saying, in dream state, "Emm, excuse me, you're not (my beloved's name) you don't have permission to be here. I remember waking up and knowing exactly who it was even though they hid their face in my dream.

One night I did something totally different. While I was dreaming, I was very conscious that I was dreaming a dream and I could hear my subconscious saying things like, *but this is not what you want to manifest so don't feel into it too much.* Then I would get to a scene and analyze the dream while it's going on; for example, I saw myself in a building with walls and it felt 'closed-in'. My subconscious went *ok Bernice what's this feeling of being boxed in? What is the psychology behind seeing yourself in these walls?* So, as I dreamed, I reminded myself no matter what happens here you're protected and nothing can happen because you control this.

My dreams became very vivid as time went on.

A few months later, I dreamed a dream in a dream. What I mean is, I fell asleep, and in my dream, I fell asleep again and dreamed a dream (most beautiful dream) then I woke up and said to myself *oh wow I just woke up in my dream and now I must wake up in real life.*

It's quite fascinating. I like being a conscious dreamer. I'm not the only one who has had these experiences and even more.

The next morning I asked my Higher Self what dreams are (I usually ask these questions during meditation: I focus on the question I ask and wait for the answer) I heard inside me *you're good with words Bernice go ahead and figure it out.* As I stared at the word the letters DRAMES came into focus. I was prompted to look it up in the dictionary and what I found was interesting. "Drames" is the French word for "Drama." Just like life, dreams are part of the drama of life. Play your part, enjoy, have fun and if you don't like the story/movie change it, or just go with the flow. To change your script/story, usually, all you need is a change in consciousness/awareness.

We are masters when we allow the flow of life from our hearts without resistance. We need not do as much as we need just BE. Therein lies the magic of it all.

-BERNICE ANGOH

DREAMS & REMOTE VIEWING

I had the most fascinating thing happen to me on another occasion... it wasn't a dream because I was aware of it happening, though my eyes were closed, and my body relaxed as though in sleep.

So here's what happened. One afternoon, I decided to take a little late nap. A few seconds after I closed my eyes I started seeing/feeling myself lift off my body and floating. I floated far off into the galaxies. As I drifted, I heard laughter and fiddling. It was coming from all these beautiful, shining stars and lights around me... I soon realized that I was the stars and lights, I was one of them and they were part of me... just floating as one with/in the cosmos. It was such an indescribable feeling of oneness. I no longer could tell where my body ended or where the stars began. A feeling of not only being an extension of... but a sense of the entire universe residing within me. Before long I heard, "This is who you are." As if to say, "You're not just this body... you are the universe".

I got a little nervous as I felt myself drifting off farther and deeper into the cosmos, so I thought *I must return,* and immediately I was back in myself (body). Though my eyes had been closed for just a few minutes throughout this experience, it felt like I was gone for hours. It was exhilarating.

Later, I was talking to a friend (who is now my husband) on the phone, and I saw him as if he were in front of me, though he was 5,000 miles away in the U.K. As we were talking, right in the middle of the conversation, I found myself in front of him watching him talk to me on the phone... then all of a sudden I was out of the scene. When I started to describe to him in detail what I had seen: what he was wearing (the color and style), how he was seated, his posture and how his legs were positioned ...

He almost hung up on me, as he too was floored by what had just taken place. He said it sent chills down his spine as I had described exactly word for word how he was, his posture, how his legs were positioned, and exactly what he was wearing. He said, "How the heck did you know that!" I told him I had just visited him-- unintentionally.

I had several unexplained experiences like that but usually they come as a memory of a real event which has been or is yet to take place. That day was one of the rare instances when I saw someone in 'real time' as it was happening—even though they were in another country.

Wanting leaves no room for surprises. Allowing opens hidden doors with hidden treasures for your delight.

~BERNICE ANGOH

Sometimes the universe waits until we know we're worthy of the thing we desire before it gives it to us.

~BERNICE ANGOH

BELIEVING IT IN...

There's not one of us here who hasn't told a lie or two. When it was convenient, we found a way to get out of a state by bearing false information.

If you can lie, you can imagine!

If you've ever faked it, (a smile, an orgasm, whatever...) you can imagine!

You are all-natural actors anyway. You wake up every day in this world and act; you play a part. Some are wives, others are mothers, others pretend to like their jobs or their colleagues. Shakespeare once said, "All the world's a stage..." and we're all just playing a role.

When you were a child and you got in trouble, I bet your first instinct was to find a way to get out of trouble! See? It's innate, we all can and know how to get out of one state into another.

The phrase "fake it till you make it" is exactly that.

As a child we used to play "house" and I remember putting clothes under my dress to insinuate I was pregnant and making my own dolls out of straw or excess fabric.

WE ARE CREATORS! We have always been and always will be! Creativity is the only thing that slows time down or makes it non-existent. Because in the moment of creating we are at out full potential, we are most godlike. Catch yourself when you're doing something you enjoy doing. Do you realize how lost into the act we are? We have fun because we are at play. Life is play.

When did we forget this? When did we start to fear to 'make up' our own stories and bask in the state? You did this as a child all the time and often too! And when you did, you enjoyed the feeling, and it became real to you... and usually we dropped it and resumed the next day and next for how long we wanted to continue enjoying that state. What's the difference now? There's none except your mind and old patterns.

So yes, there you have it. Go back to being childlike, enjoy being and doing the thing that comes easily to you. When you strike the balance between envisioning your dream and being content now, you have opened the portal to endless possibilities.

Let the "acting" begin. Your Oscar will be given to you in this physical realm as your very own desire materialized.

But you are already that which you desire to be NOW. You are full of all possibilities there is.

All our desires are like babies... so don't worry when or how that 'baby' is being created, it's not you who puts the hair on the babies' head or puts his/her fingernails.

Think, do I want my 'baby' full term and healthy as possible or do I want a premature baby? So, stop worrying about it taking 'too long' your 'baby' is being perfected inside of you... SAY THANK YOU AND STAY THANKFUL...in its appointed time you will behold your 'babies'.

When things SEEM to be falling apart, don't fret, don't panic... Be excited instead; assist in the 'emptying' so that when you're being filled, eventually, every 'clean' corner can be reached. There is no emptying without a filling up, no night without day, no hurt without healing, all is as it should be: beautiful in complexity and simplicity.

-BERNICE ANGOH

Giving is receiving.

~BERNICE ANGOH

IMAGINE LOVINGLY FOR OTHERS

I wish I could tell of all the manifestations galore happening in and around my life. I am so overwhelmed with joy, and ever still amazed when it all happens.

Many months ago, I talked to my dearest aunt who was told me of all her struggles and burdens. She is such a beautiful soul and kind to the core. I decided to think lovingly for her.

I imagined for my aunt to have a decent job so she can stay in the country she was in. (Her job contract was over, and she had gone for months without work.)

I also saw her happy in love with a man who loves and spoils her ...

First, she reported to me that she had soon gotten a better contract job for another year, and later that week she told me she'd met a sweet, wealthy, and kind-hearted man who spoils her.

The excitement in her voice made me smile. I didn't tell her of anything I did.

Letting go is an act of kindness to oneself; it is accepting that you are more than enough and loving yourself enough to remain free and non-attached.

~BERNICE ANGOH

HEALING YOURSELF BY LOVING OTHERS

Think lovingly of others. What you want or wish for others, you're wishing for yourself. Think of them lovingly and let it go. Don't linger or be attached waiting to see if something happens.... that's the secret, imagine and let go...it's part of unconditional loving.

I did something during meditation. I was so filled with love, and I thought of a few people I could send it to; people with whom I had been estranged from or had lost communication with.

My ex and were on nice terms, we talked about our children, but that was usually it. I thought I should send him love energy because I cared for him as a human… and someone I once was in love with enough to birth my beautiful children with.

During meditation I called him to my awareness and said over and over, "I'm sorry, please forgive me, I love you, thank you". I was reciting the Ho-opono-pono. I was so moved uttering those sacred words, that I began to cry. And then I whispered, "I love you always."

Next, I did the same for a family member of mine with whom I'd not spoken for a while. Our highest communication was, "Hi" and "Hope you're well," just out of courtesy because we shared the same blood. I closed my eyes and called her higher self to my awareness, and again, recited the Ho-opono-pono, "I'm sorry please forgive, I love, thank you."

Next, I had a colleague with whom I hadn't talked for several months over some disagreement. With him I just thought *oh, I should reach out to him and break this silence.* I remembered his kindness and what an amazing person he was. That's all I did and then I forgot all about it.

Later that evening, this family member of mine tagged me on some funny video on Facebook and I thought well isn't that something! She barely reaches out to me, even when in the past I'd been the one reaching out to mend things. But She felt my energy, and the video was quite hilarious. It made me smile.

Hours later, I got a text from my colleague and while I was reconnecting with him my ex sends me a sweet message asking how I'm doing.... I thought WOW!

We had the most caring conversation, my ex and I, and my colleague and I got back on track like nothing ever happened.

There was one or two other people I called to mind and said either "Please forgive me, I love you" or "I forgive you and I love you," based on what the situation of our relationship was.

Being loving not only frees you, but it also heals you, and heals the other.

After this experience I thought well, how is that for taking every part of yourself and healing from inside!

I also send love to the entire world. We are beings of love, we are love itself... let your love not end with you, your needs/desires or those around you.... it is important to start with Self yes, but go a little further, take all the love in your heart and pour it over another, feel for them like it was your one main desire! Think lovingly of, and for them, and in so doing you'll heal parts of you and open yourself for more love to flow in.♥

EXUDE THAT WHICH YOU WANT TO BEHOLD

I remember doing something similar a couple of years ago when my ex was not being very respectful or kind to me verbally and emotionally. We were not together, yet there was so much strain and strife in our relationship. I thought, *I can't continue with this man like this, we need to be civil and amicable for the benefit of us and our kids.*

I decided to change my perception of him in my mind. Instead of calling him names in my mind and thinking he was a loser, I started to bless him and speak words of love over him. I remembered that he was someone's child, and that he was very loved by his parents. I remembered that he was acting from his own level of consciousness which had little to do with me. Lastly, I remembered the little boy in him was wounded, the one who was, and still was trying to make his own path in this world. Exactly three days after whispering all these prayers and intentions over him, he became a completely different person! I was dumbfounded. I mean a 360 degree change from being a bully to being extremely kind and respectful towards me in words and deed.

Slowly you can heal those around you when you change your perception of them in your mind. Do it wholeheartedly from a place of love and I swear they will bloom around you like roses in a beautiful rose garden.

Life is an echo, everything comes from you,
and everything returns to you.

~BERNICE ANGOH

MANIFESTING A SPECIFIC PARTNER
(HOW I GOT MY EX BACK)

I've told this story so many times, and each time, even I am in awe of how it unfolded. This happened several years ago when I was still highly indoctrinated and didn't know about manifestation. I just had a strong belief and I wanted it so very badly.

I had married the same man twice and we have two children. It was one of those relationships that had reached its point of letting go.

I was the one who walked away each time. I wanted more out of life, and I knew there was something much more beautiful waiting for me, so I followed my intuition.

After the second time we married and had our son, I decided to let go once again. We were separated for over two years and barely talking, except when it came to our children.

While the divorce was pending, I dated for a brief period. He too had a girlfriend in the city he lived in.

My daughter's wish that Christmas was for me to give her dad one more chance so we could have the family together. I looked at my daughter and something moved inside me, because in her I saw my

12-year-old self who wished my parents had never divorced. So, I said yes and promised her I would not give up until her dad came home.

Of course it was a surprise to everyone since we had been living in different cities for over two years. When he heard my wish, he said, "Over my dead body, I will never ever be crazy enough to get back with her!"

I was determined. I went out and bought frames and put pictures of my ex-husband and I in them. There were no pictures on my wall before, but I made the change to put up our photos all over the house. I printed family pictures and placed them everywhere in every room of the house. It looked like a family lived there. Next, I pushed my clothes to one side of the closet and made space for his clothes when he would return. When we ate dinner, I put a plate for him at the table. I wrote encouraging words on the mirrors and put my wedding ring back on.

I was alone in this, well, me and my daughter. His parents didn't want a part of it. He had even taken the girl, he was seeing at the time, to his parents for Christmas dinner, and she had bought expensive gifts for my kids. It hurt so much that I cried.

I decided to call her and ask her to step aside while I tried to work things out with my children's father, and she very confidently told me there was nothing I could ever do to separate the two of them. Oh, how that made me angry! I said to myself, *B*tch we will just have to see about that!*

As time went on, things seemed to be getting worse. He visited her parents and family and moved in with her! Before long I heard they were engaged. Every little news I heard broke my heart. I almost gave up, but I was encouraged by my faith, plus I didn't want to break the promise I made to my daughter.

One day, I was served with divorce papers from him. I looked at it, smiled, and burned it! He was furious when he heard what I'd done. The worse things got, the more I started to feel things were going great in the spiritual realm. I had become this person who loved unconditionally. I stopped insulting the other woman when I talked about her, and completely forgave her and my children's father too. All I had was endless love and compassion. It was so intense that it surprised even me. I had gotten so much closer to God and reached the point when I said "...even if he doesn't come back, I'm richer in love than I was before I began this journey."

But I didn't give up, I kept saying, **"Just watch, he won't even take a plane to come here, he will get into his truck and drive all the way from where he is to my front door!"**

I even did the Esther fast! Yes, I went for three days and night without food and water, all the while working a 12-hour shift every night at the children's hospital. It was intense, and something I had never attempted—nor will ever do again.

There was a 'hiring' sign right next to where I lived and each time, I drove by I wondered, *geez it's been months and that sign is still there!* One day while driving with my daughter I said, **"You see that sign? That job is waiting for your father!"**

During this period I had so many wonderful things happen to me; visions and all. I wrote in my journal every day. **One day, while I prayed, I felt that I should make a sign that said, "Welcome home daddy"**. The children and I made a beautiful sign and hung it in the living room.

I remember one afternoon singing joyfully and feeling so much joy, as if my heart exploded within. I told my friend, "It is done! I feel it is done!"

Two days later I wrote a note in my journal that said, "My husband is coming home tonight ...."

The very next day around 4pm, my phone rang. It was him. Mind you, we had barely spoken through the years! Most of the times his parents transmitted his message. I stared at my phone in shock and picked it up.

The voice on the other end said, "I just want to tell you that I am coming home. I am driving in my truck and not sure how long it will take me to get there. I don't even have enough gas in my truck but I'm coming home."

All I said was, "I love you." And he replied, "I love you too". Words I never thought I'd ever hear again. This is the same man who said he will never ever get back with me. **He had left work that morning and not even returned to collect his belongings from the house he shared with his girlfriend. He drove for 24 hours all the way to my front door, with just the clothes on his back.**

When he came in, he was very overwhelmed to see the house looking as though he lived there. The children were happy, and so was I.

When he went job hunting a few weeks later, he applied to three jobs including the one I said was going to be his. **The only job that accepted and hired him was the one I had declared.**

These are the few details I can share, but there are so many more. All this happened within six months.

A closed heart is limited in its capacity to love. A heart that has been broken is open to receive and to give more love.

-Bernice Angoh

p.s We are not together anymore. I ended it for good reasons. Someday soon I will tell you, for there was an even greater unfolding about to happen...

***This incident with my children's dad was very karmic for me. Because at one point, while physically separated from my children's dad and pursuing a divorce, I had very briefly, and unknowingly, dated someone who was married. This person was one of my close friends who I had no reason to believe he was lying when he said he and his wife were not together anymore and were talking about divorce. I naively believed what he said because he was my best friend since childhood, but truth is, I should've still said no. It was a very shameful period in my life.

So, I say this incident with my children's dad was karmic for me because I got to experience the pain the other woman went through when I believed my-then-best-friend. This allowed me to have compassion for the woman my children's dad was dating—as I was once in her place--and also to show compassion for him. I had learned that whatever you do (knowingly or unknowingly) usually comes back to you. Not to punish you, but to humble you to open your heart for more love, kindness, and less judgement.

I had the fortunate opportunity to talk this ex-best-friend's wife. She asked to talk to me, and having nothing to hide, I accepted. We talked for hours, and even laughed over certain things. It was the beginning of healing for me, and I suppose for her as well.

In the case against love, I choose to see only the pros:
If it's unfavorable, it forces us to change. If it's favorable,
it causes us to bloom.

~BERNICE ANGOH

LIFE IS YOUR PANTRY

You live in a house, and you have a limitless pantry; your 3D self or your "meat suit" is you and your higher self is the pantry (just for analogy's sake). Your higher self is an aspect of you which understand things more than you do, things beyond what you can physically perceive.

Now, who put the pantry in that house that contains everything? You of course because it's your house. It's so vast you can't see some of the things you stocked up way in the back... you think oh, I don't have it, but higher self knows better, she knows you have it in there. Now, this is when you ask higher self, aka, subconscious to 'bring it forth' by imagining you already have it.

If it is for your highest good, it will eventually manifest in the physical. Whatever you want, you must ask first and then relax about it. You cannot want it a certain way because you don't know HOW it may choose to come about.

WHERE TWO OR MORE ARE GATHERED...

CO-CREATING AT ITS BEST!

It's always fun co-creating with someone. A friend and I had been creating way before we ever met each other in the physical. We wrote and published a book together, created a company and some other fun, personal things. As a dance instructor, one of her wishes was to meet with Shaun T (International renowned fitness instructor and author).

We had conversations about this on several occasions, like we do with everything else in life and we were excited about. One morning we decided to 'manifest' this desire. We both laid down on our couches, she in Virginia and I in Arkansas. After our routine of relaxation and imagination, I asked her what she 'saw' in her imagination. She said, "I saw myself calling you to tell you I'd met Shaun T." She then asked me what I saw, and I replied," You were on stage dancing with Shaun T and the crowd of people watching were going wild." We laughed, carried on our conversation with other matters and then got off the phone.

Exactly nine months after, when we'd both forgotten all about that phone call, she called me screaming into the phone, "Guess who I met today in North Carolina!" Of course, I could already guess, but it was what she said next that had tears rolling down my face.

"I danced on stage with Shaun T. I showed up at some fitness event while in North Carolina and guess who was there? He asked a question and when I raised my hand to explain how I got back my toned figure after three babies, he called me on stage to show him some dance moves!"

Just as I'd seen it in my imagination. She could've met him at an airport, or a grocery store or any place else, but no, she danced with him on a stage with a crowd watching, recording, and going wild as they danced.

And yes, she did call me excitedly to tell me the news, just like in her imagination.

THE WITNESS

I AM, THAT I AM

I was meditating and I got so relaxed that I became detached from my physical body. I heard my own body on the bed breathing but felt like it was separate from the one listening. I remember thinking *Oh, look at her breathing, such a nice, peaceful sound.* At the same time, I asked *who are you, who is listening then to Bernice breathing?* Of course, I knew the answer to the question.

This happened because I'd been realizing more and more that I AM!

KNOWing that everything is happening for my/your highest good leaves no room for self-pity, sadness, bitterness, or anger. When you get to the point when you can say, "Ah, hello there, Pain, my friend, what good gifts are you bringing for me this time?" When you get to that point, you have embodied the art of true surrender, letting go and allowing.

Allowing is the revolving door of manifestations
~ **Bernice Angoh**

Do you know what you'd like for yourself? See yourself ecstatic. Pay attention to your intuition, then act accordingly. Of course, there will be certain things you think are best for you that will elude you. I will address that later when we talk about grace. Unfortunately, we live this third dimensional world where the power struggle is evident. Even when we have enough to go around, some people still go without. But the goal is to focus on the good we can do in our own little way.

Change the way you look at things—it's all about perception. Your thinking stems from your beliefs.... your beliefs stem from your upbringing (environment).

Start to shift your beliefs by feeding your mind with new material... once your beliefs change your actions and self-talk will follow suit .... seems easier to write, but it's well worth it to do.

Be still and KNOW that I AM! Not I was or I am going to be, but I AM; all past and future converge in the present moment

When you say or read that statement aloud, you're referring to yourself. Say it boldly because you are that! You are pure consciousness. You're talking to your mind and saying, "Be still my mind... I AM God/Love!" Or "Be still my heart, you have no reason to be anxious, I AM God/Love, remember?" Almost in a cheeky kind of way like why the heck are you even bothered by these little nonsensical things in 3D world?

Other statements you can say out loud are: "I AM the resurrection, I AM the truth, I AM the life!"

"I AM the prophecy fulfilling itself."

"I AM love multiplied, amplified and interacting with itself."

"I AM invincible, immortal, eternal."

"I AM enough!"

Just a few...

The more you speak it, the more you start to feel the power! When I say it, I know it is my truth, it is the ONLY truth.

You must be quiet loud enough
to hear your soul speak.

-BERNICE ANGOH

MEDITATION: ACCESSING YOUR HIGHER SELF

When I started meditating, I was clueless. My mind wouldn't quiet down. It takes practice, and before you know meditation becomes you!

I would fall asleep sometimes and never follow through with my guided meditation. I almost gave up many times.

The first meditations I used to do were guided meditations by DavidJi on SoundCloud.

The key with meditation is to be relaxed, you don't have to sit in the lotus position if its uncomfortable. I lay down flat on my back most of the time.

Focus on your breathing! Breathing is everything when it comes to meditation, after all your breath is Spirit....Feel it come in and go out. Usually I say in my mind 'I' as I inhale and 'AM' as I exhale. With your eyes closed, focus them on the space between your eyebrows (Ajna chakra or third eye)

Like I said, it is practice. Let thoughts come and go, watch them come in through a 'door' and 'exit' through another 'door' (all in your mind). You are not these thoughts—they are merely visitors. Which of them you choose to let in and entertain you is entirely up to you. The real you is always observing. The real you (higher self) is silent/silence.

Using my mantras also helped me a lot.

Music is my favorite form of transpiration.

I am always catapulted into a world where I am music itself—and I feel at home. Find your style, find what relaxes you: some people prefer quiet, some prefer to light candles and some burn incense ...

No matter what, be comfortable. Start in a quiet space or make a space in your house which is your sacred space.

Many times, I would see myself shrouded in celestial light. Either basking in it or sending it to others and into the world.

Eventually meditation not only becomes those segments of the day you cut out to go away for a while, but it becomes you. When you become aware and conscious of every moment, YOU are PRESENT. That is meditation.

When you become fully love, unconditional love, that's meditation... love is the ultimate meditation. Your most natural state is love. So then, you're always in meditation.

When you come to the realization that life's unpredictability is far more compassionate than what you've planed or cooked up in your imagination, you'll finally be free to let go.

-BERNICE ANGOH

SURRENDER

To surrender is to create; surrender is the most natural form of creation…

We all know that we are God, but so many confuse the physical self to be God. It is consciousness which is the God-part of us. The life force: the great spirit/energy that flows through us. It is that which brings about all we think are mere coincidences.

Unconditional love and surrender are synonymous. Trust and surrender are also synonymous. People do all they can, they imagine and visualize but then they reach the point of letting go or surrendering and they get stuck because ego kicks in and they want to be in control.

Refusing to surrender is like going to a store to buy something, but when the salesclerk wraps it up, puts it in front of you and says, "That will be $$$", you stand there afraid to give the money because you're scared to lose the money you have. At least that's the way I look at it.

You think letting go or surrendering means you'll not get your manifestation, but it's the other way around. It is not a power trip. It is giving in to something greater than yourself. It is trusting the unknown. If you don't learn these lessons, the road will seem torturous and long for you. Your physical person can do NOTHING except follow inspired actions when you're compelled to. Don't fool yourself! What great accomplishment have you made by just your physical self?

Are you the one who tells yourself to breathe, or do you just breathe involuntarily? Do you tell your heart to beat or how much blood your veins circulate at any given time? DO you wake yourself up in the morning, or tell the winter when to arrive? Humble yourself, trust is part of humility; surrender is part of humility.

Unless a grain of wheat dies it remains alone... Die to this fake self you believe is the sh*t, it is awesome to have these bodies but don't make them an idol, they are simply vessels through which the divine expresses itself. Die to the old man and the old way of being. A change in consciousness is a change in your story. Learn to be patient, it is a superpower. Learn to surrender/let go, the bravest people know that's their superpower.

You say you're tired and in pain, that you're frustrated because things are not happening as you wish or as quickly as you'd want... well then, relieve yourself of the 'burden' and surrender. Why are you trying to carry a 'load' which is not yours to carry?

You must learn to TRUST completely; there is no glory without SURRENDER. What can your mere flesh do? Everything is consciousness. You're here in this physical form as a witness and an observer. You're here to receive, and who is the giver? You guessed it; I AM (your Higher Self).

The main purpose of our lives is to learn unconditional love, to remember that we are love itself. Love is a self-fulfilling prophecy. Nothing comes to you but by Divine Love. Is there someone you need to forgive? Forgive them and let it go. Do you need to forgive your own self? Then do it! Take time and look at your own self, ask your higher self to guide you and he/she will. This is your toiling and your planting, and in time your harvest will be rich. But you must trust as the farmer trusts that the sun will make his plants grow and the rain will water his fields. He doesn't go screaming at the sun or gets frustrated at the clouds... he trusts and knows that if he has done his part the rest will follow.

Also, turn away from your own wants and be of help to others. What you want, give!

When I was younger, I used to sing these songs during periods of my life when I had to surrender...

"I cast all my cares upon you. I lay all of my burden down at your feet and anytime I don't know what to do, I will cast all my cares upon you."

Another one:

"In his time, he makes all things beautiful in his time, lord please show me every day as you're teaching me always that you'll do just what you say in your time. In your time you make all things beautiful in your time, lord my life to you I bring may each song I have to sing be to you a lovely beam in your time."

According to esoteric Christianity the "Lord" we are talking about is your Higher Self, that part of you that is Divine and connected to the Source of all things. That part of you is Love. I learned that the bible is far from literal. Personally, I believe it would have been to our best interest had we been taught esoteric interpretations of whatever religions we were born into. It helps to be open-minded enough to know you don't know everything, to study all the different religions, and to know that no one knows the absolute truth. Understanding religious texts, the way they were meant to be understood opened up the human experience for me. And till date, the more I learn, the more I realize I know very little.

If you're not a religious person, you can replace the words like so: "In your time, you make all things beautiful, in your time. Love, please show me every day..."

Again, do not worry how or when. In the appointed time your desires will materialize in the physical world. In the meantime, remember to not focus on the effect (physical reality, unless it matches with what you want). Your subconscious is the causation. It is there you pluck the weeds, by thinking on the good things you want for yourself.

Be thankful. When something happens that is not in sync with what you desire, say "Thank You", for that very circumstance is the path leading to the 'appearance' of your desire.

Have a heart for humanity... this is the difference; the love in you changes everything in its path. You cannot love one living thing and despise the other. Your love should include all beings.

And sometimes love involves fighting for what is just and right. Love involves looking evil in the eye and calling it for what it is. Love is not always docile. Sometimes love is a burning, roasting, destroying-to-rebuild fire.

Finally, remember your desire comes with its ways of fulfilling itself.

ACCEPTING THE MOMENT AS IS

I learned a valuable lesson through painful experiences about how and why it is necessary to accept certain things as they are and why it is important to flow with life. With so much talk of manifesting, I started to realize that there was some ego-trip about the entire process. I had to purify my ego, I had to let go of attachment to things and people.

At one time I was living 90% in imagination and 10% in the now. I was very much unbalanced, and I refused to acknowledge it for a while. With it came suffering, because I thought I could control everything, even people. What's the joy in knowing you try to manipulate someone's emotions to favor your selfish need? There's no fun in that, and it takes out the organic nature and flow of life. But since we are still novices, the universe allows us to have fun and sometimes we get what we desperately want even when it's not the best thing for us. Such experiences end up humbling us the most as we experience needless suffering and pain until at last, we let go.

Sometimes some of us need many scenarios until we get it. Ever wondered why it feels like your life is never changing for the better, and why it feels like you keep finding yourself in the same painful situations or with the same challenging partners/relationships? I have seen people stay in horrible situations and allowed others to treat them horribly because they're convinced that person is their soulmate. Heck, I've been one of those people.

The key to life is accepting every moment as it is, as if you set it up for yourself to experience. But don't linger in suffering. As you become increasingly aware, it gets easier to let things and people go. Your satisfaction doesn't come from a specific person or situation. It comes from an endless well within: Source/Love.

A good indication of how much you've grown
is by how easily you let things go
~Bernice Angoh

When you accept every moment as is, all pain and suffering dissipate, every yearning and desire dissolves. This is the perfect state of being in which we don't seek to manifest, we become the manifested.

KARMA & RELATIONSHIPS

Relationships are not only the best growth indicators; they are the best growth instigators.

No one is an island. We cannot survive without relating. Because everyone you meet is a mirror, you will always meet who you are. We are all just interacting with ourselves. That is why one affects the whole, and why what you do to another, you do unto yourself. This is the reason every philosopher and mystic that ever lived stressed about treating your neighbor as yourself. In short, we are all "Mirrors" and life is this beautiful kaleidoscope of all our thoughts and emotions bouncing back and forth.

Karma to me is just an opportunity to be more compassionate and loving rather than a payback system (insinuating revenge). People you meet are your teachers and we learn most from some of the painful relationships we've had. If you don't learn what you must learn to be more of who you are (love) you will meet the same kind of people with the same baggage you carry in your subconscious. Relationships are a fantastic opportunity for expanding our awareness and purifying the ego, because if you can see yourself in another, there is an immense potential for kindness and empathy. Most of the drama we see in others is simply the drama within us asking to change the story. So, when you are no longer with someone, bless them and wish them well. This is how you change the story within you, and when you do, you begin to reflect a much more peaceful disposition. Your light is not just for your feet as you walk your path, your light reflects and lights up others' paths as well.

Learn to forgive yourself and the other person when a relationship ends; it may sting in the beginning but eventually, hopefully, you remember that the person is simply another you. You can forgive without associating any further with a particular person. You can love and be happy for another even if their happiness does not include your participation.

Most importantly, when relationships end and people are removed from your circle, it may be their higher self and yours conspiring to free you—and/or them-- from each other's karmic cycle. It allows you to be free from any toxic soul ties, soul contracts or cords that no longer serve a purpose. This in turn provides both parties the opportunity to continue, independently, on their path of expansion.

If you look back at the relationships you've had you will see how valuable each experience was; nothing is ever in vain, every pain is a gain.

THE LETTING GO PRAYER
(HO'OPONOPONO REVISED)

Thank you for joining me on this journey
However long or brief it may have been
I appreciate you showing up in my life when you did
And if there's any residual pain or hurt
I'm sorry
Please forgive me
I love you
Thank you.

The reason some of us have a challenging time letting go is because we've let the pain become a source of comfort to us so much so that we're not sure we can survive without it.

~BERNICE ANGOH

LETTING GO

Surrender is simply another word for trust. Sometimes when people hear the word surrender they feel they have to DO something but it's the exact opposite, you DO NOTHING and just BE!

You, me, all of us are basically walking prayers... we speak and it's done, we imagine and visualize and it's done, but we have a hard time believing it's that simple so we do like we've been trained to do; we try to make it happen using unnecessary effort. But I tell you, unless it's inspired action, do nothing. Once you've done your part, let go and allow the universe/consciousness to do its own. Do not try to help it, you'll just be putting obstacles in your own path. I learned this the hard way--don't we all?

Our very nature is surrender; we must remember to let it be! Let it go. You don't write a letter and not mail it! Do you? You're confident that the mail carrier will take it and not tear it on the way... then trust the universe a little more! The secret here is having unconditional love for everyone and all things. Some may ask how do you do that? Ask your higher self, have a relationship with him/her. Whatever I want I ask my higher self and she always reveals it to me in some way.

So, yes, prayers/intentions are answered by the powers we invoke and not by powers we exert (doing something)

Imagine. Feel. Be. =Experience.

MONEY & ABUNDANCE

I had exactly one month to move from one state to another. It was a move I was excited about because it was a chance for a new opportunity. After much calculating, I realized I needed much more money to start off right. I needed $3,000 to pay my rent three months in advance. My bank account was empty, but I knew I was moving no matter what. I continued to pack as though I already had the money. Two weeks came and went. And nothing happened. I figured, what will be will be. I wasn't as anxious or nervous as I usually would be.

One morning, on the third week, I received a message from a stranger on Facebook. He began by saying how much he loved my poems and my shamanic wisdom. Apparently, he was subscribed to my Facebook poetry page. He then added, "Do you know of any editors? I have a book that needs editing." I replied, "I am an editor." He quickly responded, "Oh, I was hoping you would say that, because you'd be the perfect person to work on my book, especially since it deals with themes of spirituality and mysticism. It would be an honor to have someone with your insights work on my book." I was flattered, not just because he was much, much older, and wiser, but that he didn't want anyone else editing his book. He asked that we start soon, and I agreed. He emailed me the manuscript so I could give him a quote. To be honest, it needed a lot of work, but it was work I was happy to do. I replied with a quote of $3,500. He sent the money immediately.

While editing, I realized he was once a famous actor. He not only allowed me the liberty to edit as I saw fit, but he also consulted with me for other decisions in the publishing process, including the image for the book cover. His acknowledgment page had my name and a thank you paragraph. When the book was published, he left me one of the most glowing reviews I'd received on his Facebook page. That review got me my next client.

With every major heart surgery, there is a healing period. Heartbreak is no different. Letting go is not the healing period, it is only the surgery…now the healing will begin.

-BERNICE ANGOH

THE LIST GUY
(THE LESSON)

I still remember, many years ago, screaming to the universe to send someone who loves like I do. I said, "In all this vast universe, there has to be someone out there just for me, someone who loves infinitely as I do." Well, it wasn't long before my friend, Mercy, sent me a text asking me to write down one hundred traits of the person I'd like to end up with. I told her I just wanted an evolved guy. She said she wanted me to try and list as many characteristics as I could. At first, I thought I'd end up with just ten, but I wrote down 98—surprisingly.

A few weeks later, I got a friend's request from a friend of a friend on Facebook. I sensed his entry into my vibrational field and wondered what he was there for and why. I was that way with everyone I encountered. I knew nothing was by accident. Soon, he started commenting and liking my photos and next thing you know, he began messaging me. He was quite into me early on which was a red flag, but I ignored it. I was very skeptical and kept it at an amicable level. He was a Sivananda yoga teacher and a financial adviser. He was older than me, by 13 years, and he was quite the charmer.

The more we communicated the more I started to like him. Somehow, he worked his way into my resisting heart through his poetry and stories. I thought he could be the person who would be most compatible with me on a soul level. But no sooner had he confessed his love and built all these dreams in my head, than they began to crumble. Things got interesting. I explain more of how we met and the story behind how I came to understand what the term "Twin Flame" meant through our meeting. The whole experience set in motion a series of events even I couldn't have predicted. I write further about these series of magical experiences in my upcoming poetry/short story series titled "IN ONE BREATH." You can purchase all the volumes through my site www.berniceangoh.com or stay posted on my social media sites, especially tiktok (@iam_magic9)

This relationship helped me learn one of the biggest lessons in my life, that of letting go. It also taught me a most valuable lesson about manifesting; the desire comes through you to fulfill its purpose, whatever it is that you think you're manifesting is already something that was going to happen anyway. When things come, let them come and when they go, let them go. Some people will learn, grow, expand, and ascend to higher levels of consciousness in this lifetime, but others, stubborn and ego-driven, will repeat the same lessons in different lifetimes until they get it.

The relationships we hold on to long after they're over, are usually the ones that were there to teach us how to let go.

-BERNICE ANGOH

EGO PLAY

There is a thin line between knowing who you are and still allowing for ego to control you. Many people become enslaved by the ego once more when they find out that they are co-creators of their own reality. They want to learn and master 'the techniques' of 'manifesting' and get so distracted and forget to live in the moment. They forget that 'manifesting' is innate.

No one taught you as a child how to imagine and make-believe or how to feel excited about something you really desired or wished for. As a child, I remember always saying, "Oh, how nice it would be if…" or "I wish I could have…" there was so little resistance. There is a thin line between being confident and being egotistically boastful. "I can have whatever the hell I please!" I've heard some people say. I may have even said so myself at some point. They are willing to hurt people in the process of getting what they selfishly desire. I've seen some people talk about learning techniques to break up a happy couple just so they can have the man to themselves. They usually are not coming from a place of love, and as far as I've experienced, Love has no room for anything but humility. Confidence is acknowledging that the creative power within you has a way of bringing to you what you need. Confidence makes room for Grace, boasting does not.

Imagine a little child pouting and throwing a tantrum because they want what they want and will not take no for an answer from their mother. Whenever the mother tries to explain why that thing or situation may not serve them most, they deny and throw an even worse fit. Finally, the mother decides to give in, so that they will experience the contrast of not trusting. There is an African proverb that says, *"What a young man can't see standing, an old man can see sitting down."*

The loving Mother is your Higher-self. The old man is your Higher-self. You came to this life to experience certain things and you will; if you delay them, you will meet them again until you learn and grow spiritually from what that experience was meant to teach you.

"When the ego is purified, the soul flourishes."
~Marc Lee

The ego doesn't have to be destroyed, there is a reason it's there in the first place; to serve you. The only thing that can purify the ego is love and love is our 'goal.' Until we learn how to cultivate a healthy ego, we will be distracted, continuously, from our path. The best way I know to cultivate a healthy ego is through acceptance and learning how to let go.

When I became known as a "Master manifester," I began to realize how much I enjoyed that people looked up to me. I quickly caught myself and checked my ego. Humans love to worship and follow; they make gods of anyone who is succeeding in something a little more than they are. When I started to notice that people saw me this way, I had to remember that I wasn't any more of a teacher than they were. We were both teacher and student, I just had a better understanding of things through experience. I always referred them back to themselves, by giving them the tools to see within, when they reached out to me to help manifest things for them, especially their love interests. I like co-creating with clients, it can be so much fun if they grasp the concepts and are willing to grow through the process. Don't get me wrong, thoroughly enjoy helping, but I didn't want anyone putting me on some pedestal. This was important for me because I had to continuously maintain the growth I'd begun, and to keep my shoulders at the same level as everyone else.

ROOM FOR GRACE

Do you know when they say hindsight is 20/20? Or when they say be careful what you wish for? Or when someone says, "I dodged that bullet!" There is nothing wrong with ambition, nothing wrong with wanting the best for ourselves and those we care about. There is a thin line though, between ambition and greed. When ambition is laced with your passion, there is opportunity for healing and growth but when it is laced with envy and greed there will always be destruction.

Grace is divine intervention. Grace is a physical expression of Love. Grace is when you get what is best instead of what is barely good or just okay. When you have an opportunity to learn and grow, your Higher-self will indulge your selfish wants. There are things we know nothing of, a guiding force that connects all the dots and knows which way to direct us towards becoming the best version of ourselves, which is Love.

All of life is Love in expression.

We are never lost, we just delay things because of resistance, attachment, and refusal to surrender, let go and flow.

Do you remember those moments in life when it seemed like a miracle when some unlikely thing happened other than the results you were anticipating? That is Grace. That is Love.

Ever been held back by a phone call and missed the bus you usually take only to find out it had a little bit of an accident? That is Grace.

I suppose we've all had those missed misfortunes in our lives at one point or the other.

How do you allow for Grace? By trusting in every moment and being fully present. Grace resides in us as what we all call intuition. Everything is connected and points back to Love.

See every moment and everyone as a messenger.

See every lesson as a gift.

Trust, Surrender and Grace are the Holy trinity of living in the NOW.

TOO BUSY MANIFESTING

When you're busy manifesting you're not living in the moment, you're not listening to Higher Self, but are being directed by ego. What makes you so unhappy with this moment that you choose to dwell only in the 'future'? What makes you so fearful and mistrusting that you allow yourself to keep digging up the past? Creation is effortless: look at the river; look at the trees; look at the birds; look at the seasons... what burden you've decided you must carry... if you know you'll get there anyway, why choose to do it with a boulder on your shoulder?

I once was part of a group that focused on manifesting, and they had one teacher whose teachings were the only one allowed. It was all fun until I started to see how so many worshipped him as though he was the beginning and the end. They had traded one God for another and didn't even know it. I'm very sure the teacher himself wouldn't have approved of their shutting everyone out and refusing to read outside of his work. Not only that, but I found out I was more focused on "getting" most of the time. Almost everyone in the group was selfishly chasing something they wanted, and by any means necessary.

People spent their whole days practicing techniques and doing rituals to attain this thing that they so desperately wanted. I started to move away when I saw the bondage "manifesting" had become. When I let go of it, I felt free…I didn't want to trade one form of attachment for another. I wanted to be completely free in every way.

Sometimes the universe will wait until you realize
you are worth it before it gives in/it to you.

-BERNICE ANGOH

ALLOW

Allowing is a revolving door of 'entering' and 'exiting'. To truly allow, there can be no resistance or attachment. You are merely the doorway; allow for emotions to pass through you, if not, you become their prison and you, the prisoner. For emotions are ever free and somehow will exit with or without your permission. Now it's up to you if you want a peaceful exit, or a war raged against your entire being.

Allow yourself to be fully happy, loved, adored, respected, desired, appreciated etc. these are those things that never leave even if the giver/ messenger retires.

Allow yourself to cry, to let go, but without shame, guilt, judgment, self-doubt, or self-pity.

Allow for space for things even far greater than you could've imagined... Allow for these visitors like seasons' change... Experience it all, enjoy it all, indulge!

Love, love doesn't have to be like a defibrillator; to revive you every now and then. You are full of it already, and true it's so beautiful to find another whose love is as overflowing as yours, in which case there is no codependency but simply pure, unadulterated indulgence--ecstatic, bliss. A combined force of two that can transform, restore, and elevate: such is the mission of true loving, light-filled hearts.

You are the doorway but you're also timeless, selfless, and eternal: You are Love!

A time will come when you realize the only book you ever had to read was the pages of your own heart.

-BERNICE ANGOH

WISER

There was once a time in my life when I would beg, fuss, and do things hoping to make them happen and/or have people stay in my life. This is the work of the ego; denial and attachment, wanting things to be a specific way and preoccupying ourselves with futility.

When I didn't know myself, I used to not trust myself to make decisions on my own, so I sought counsel from outside sources and people whom I thought were way ahead than I was; People whose, outside, material life I thought was the standard of success. I used to think because they seemed to have 'succeeded' in life, they may know what was best for me.

I was so afraid to make the wrong decisions; ego never wants to feel small or be wrong, afraid of failing or making mistakes. Ego is control whereas love is surrendering to what is.

That went on for a long time until one day I found myself in the craziest scenario. I had a few people who held their torch lights to my flickering fire. I wouldn't let myself drown and they were my cheerleaders.

I remember one day waking up and 'hearing' in my spirit, "You beautiful, beautiful lotus!" Immediately I looked up the story of the lotus flower, and I knew that all was well with me; the 'muddy water' I was growing in was just a perfect backdrop for all that sparkled within me.

Today I am surrounded by the most beautiful of souls!

Letting go has become as automatic as breathing...

Acceptance and surrender and trust are the colors of my flag...

I'm not preoccupied with control nor wanting...

For the first time since I was a child I have learned to live here and now; not in the past which is a prison nor in the future which is an illusion...

No one dares walk over me anymore because I have truly learned to love mySELF and inevitably those people fell away...

This is the beauty of it all, that you won't have to do anything but become the truth—LOVE.

Listen to your intuition, sharpen it through meditation and your answers are always there even before you pose the question...

Leave all these things that preoccupy the mind behind; cease becoming enslaved by ideologies... watch them, play with them, but by no means be bound by them...

And amidst all your ambitions, leave room for grace.

Grace is divine intervention. A wise man, Dalai Lama, once said, "Sometimes it's by a stroke of luck that you don't get what you wanted." Beyond your imagination, there is more than just you.

Don't force things to happen. Don't try to control what you can't even perceive. Allow room for more spontaneity, and let things play out as they inevitably will. Once you have freed yourself from all attachments you will see how smoothly life will carry you to, and through, even more beautiful experiences. To truly live you cannot be attached to any ideology. This is superior living and very few get to experience it in this lifetime.

-BERNICE ANGOH

WHEN THE LESSON IS LEARNED...

Once I learned to let go and relax; once I learned to surrender and enjoy the ride; once I learned I am but the dreamer being dreamed, I started to see how everything I did before was futile. The universe will allow you to go through all your drama only to show you how futile it all is. And then you will learn the final lesson: Humility.

For the entire year after that, I began to have all sorts of people from all over the world reach out to me. Some wanted mentorship, some needed advice, and others needed a safe space to unburden. Most of these people were people I'd never met before. Some of them found me through my writing online, others through mutual friends on several social media outlets, and others through word of mouth. I heard so many "I was just drawn to your spirit, as if a magnet." One thing I sensed about all the people who reached out to me; one thing they had in common, despite their different stories, scenarios, and age, was that they were going through a lesson in the art of letting go. They just didn't know it yet, but I knew because I could see myself in each one of them. Intuitively, before some of them came to me, I'd known ahead of time they would come.

It was a much fulfilling experience to be able to teach what I had learned. Many were resistant, of course, denial is always present when ego wears the hat. For some, I spent months upon months going over certain things with them. A few walked away all together after realizing that I wasn't just going to tell them what they wanted to hear-- things that made them feel good. And for those who returned to share their testimonies with me, having finally understood what I had been saying all along, it was one of the most humbling moments for me as a guide and fellow traveler. I love to be of service because love is all I have to give.

Once the lesson is learned, new worlds emerge.

GRATITUDE

The Rebel, the Healer, the Gatekeeper & the Creator

The awakened mind views gratitude much differently than the mind which is not: one merely lists and counts the things they are grateful for as though it were a magical spell to conjure up more things for their satisfaction, while the other becomes and lives gratitude due to a deep awareness of being the source from which all things come to life.

Gratitude is an expression of appreciation or having a great attitude in whatever situation one faces. As with most things in life, there are always different views and different perspectives.

To the same truth, gratitude is the sunlight needed for all flowers of virtue to bloom.

Life as we know it would cease to exist were it not for this nine-lettered word which, ironically, is a very symbolic number in different ancient cultures.

Through my experiences, I came up with the various levels and attributes of gratitude. But before we delve into that, let us take a moment to see what a few cultures say/think about gratitude and being thankful.

Thank You

In India it is not necessary to say 'Thank you' or 'Shukriya' to friends and family because they believe friends and family are expected to be there for one another. They truly embrace the phrase 'family is everything.' To be there for those you love is their way to express gratitude and needs no recognition.

The Chinese favor gestures over words. Saying 'thank you' is easily one of the quickest ways to create a barrier between you and the people around you. Instead, it is encouraged to lose the formality and show genuine gratitude by action. The Chinese see the Westerner's overly expressed gratitude, for every little thing to be insincere. Their system of 'bao' is more of a collective than an individualistic approach to showing and expressing gratitude; what you do, you do not just for yourself but for all involved. 'Bao' means 'reciprocity;' that each act of kindness springs a debt of favorable kindness that will be returned to you in life.

If you want to show gratitude, you will really have to 'show' what you are doing for your society and how you are growing individually by building great relationships with others. It is not necessary to just say 'Thank you' or 'xiexie,' let your action have an impact.

The Mayans had a daily prayer of gratitude which they performed upon waking up. They acknowledged the seven directions of north, south, east, west, up, down and center. They believed in the blessings from nature and so they would ask permission to access the gifts that are coming to them. They asked the earth permission before ploughing the soil to plant in it, permission from a plant before harvesting it and permission from water before using it to bathe.

In ancient Kemet, where humanity's quest for closeness with the divine began, the importance of honoring the ancestral spirit was highly observed and revered. It was a way of showing gratitude for those through whom we came to be, and for who we had become through the values they left behind.

Personal hygiene, according to them, was particularly important because it directly affected spiritual cleanliness, without which any interaction with the spiritual world was impossible. Showing gratitude is a contribution; a contribution in honoring the planet and each other by always being mindful of our deeds, words, and thoughts.

The Different Levels Of Gratitude:

As with the five stages of grieving, there are four horizontal levels of gratitude and attributes that are characteristic with of an awakened mind.

The Rebel

"The Highest tribute to the dead
is not grief but gratitude."
~Thornton Wilder

It is almost impossible to feel grateful when someone you love has just passed away, when your heart is broken, or when you are starving or homeless. How can you be grateful in those times when all you want to do is take out your bleeding heart and throw it across the room? Gratitude is as fleeting as the wind in moments like these. Gratitude was never meant to be an antidote nor a placebo. Gratitude is a rebel.

In times of pain and sorrow, in moments of doubts and fear, our hearts and minds seldom move towards being grateful. When things are not going the way we planned or expected, we sometimes become very self-involved. The irony is that gratitude works the same way, except the self extends outward; it does not wallow in self-pity, blame, or shame, it rebels against those.

Gratitude is a rebel. It shows up defiantly in tough times and brings with it a legion of friends to reward the rebel. The rebel is the mother of strength and courage.

It is important to grieve and allow the emotions to pass through us; in the African culture, tears are a necessary part of cleansing any negative emotions and energies within the body. The rebelliousness of gratitude is refusing to stay in that state, but instead choosing to rise out and above it; the recognition that you have suffered enough and must find a way to live with or without the pain. The rebel finds a way to not only survive but to thrive; to be like the rose with all its thorns still in place, not as a display of self-pity but as a show of pride of having accomplished the hardest--and to shine in spite of it. The rebel does not hide his/her battle scars, they are a beautiful reminder that before every great win there is usually a great battle.

The rebel finds within the dark, the glittering stars that shine, a flicker of light worth focusing on. The rebel says 'I AM' still here and I accept this journey with all its surprises. It is at this moment that the next flower of gratitude sprouts.

The Healer, who is the mother of peace.

The Healer

"When you practice gratefulness,
there is a sense of respect towards others."
~Dalai Lama

To be grateful is to be pregnant with the fullness of NOW. Gratitude draws our attention away from worries, anxiety, depression, and uncertainties, and brings us to a place of peace. To be grateful is to be in tune with the fullness of life. And like a skill, we can practice until we not only see it as a thing to do or a way to be, but as a constant breath.

The very essence of being grateful is life. Gratitude is acknowledging those free gifts that come to you with barely or no effort on your part; like breathing. Breathing in oxygen allows for our human bodies to function properly and work like it ought. Without oxygen our organs shut down and we become diseased and slowly pass away. Gratitude is much like oxygen in that it allows for all those positive elements of joy, happiness, contentment, and peace to flow and energize our being to the point that we want to share it with others.

"No act of kindness, no matter how small, is ever wasted."
~Aesop's Fables 'The Lion and the Mouse'

To heal yourself is to heal the world. To be at peace with yourself is to be at peace with the world.

Whatever we are, the world becomes. It is not as an instantaneous process but as a ripple in the waves that are moving towards the shore.

"Neither rejoice nor lament prematurely,
for whatever may happen, all will be well if we only have health;
for happiness exists-merely in the imagination."
~Wolfgang Amadeus Mozart

Present in the Healer is also the Rebel who has gone through his/her own share of experiences and can now comfort, listen and be there for another. The Healer has finally come to one of the secrets: That all is well, and all will pass. It is not just passing through the storm but allowing the storm to pass through you to shake all the ripe 'fruits' down, discarding what doesn't belong, and moving the right things into their right places. The Healer knows that healing comes only after a hurt, and that there are no Healers without scars of overcoming. The best Healers have, at one point, been wounded. For the awakened mind, gratitude is the score in every motion picture of their life. Reminding us that even while we carry all the heavy, we can still sing through it all.

The Healer, who is the mother of peace, is also the beholder of all the puzzle pieces the Gatekeeper needs.

The Gatekeeper

"Gratitude is not only the greatest of all virtues, but the parent of all others."
~Marcus Tullius Cicero

"If awareness is the door to an abundant life, then gratitude is the gatekeeper who holds the key."
~Bernice Angoh

Being grateful and practicing gratitude is a sure way to stand before every door of this magnificent swirl called life, and to know that one door is not better than the other. All doors are full of possibilities.

Your attitude decides which room or world lies beyond. You do not go in looking for what to find, you bring with you what to 'decorate' your world with. The Gatekeeper is the mother of possibilities and adventure. The bringer of awe and wonderment.

The main strength of the Gatekeeper is to allow or to facilitate flow. Practicing gratitude allows us to give life the permission to flow through us and to give us the confidence to know that we can steer our ship across any seas.

The goal of being aware is to face every situation as an adventure. We do not go into an adventure knowing exactly how every turn will end or what we may find; knowing that takes away the joy, the anticipation and thrill. Yet in life we often do just that. Because we want to know what will happen, we do whatever we can to control the situation; life then becomes rigid and is no fun. Once this happens, we begin to complain or find ways to experience rigid-fun by seeking only those situations in which we know have a certain outcome.

The Gatekeeper is forever a child at heart, open to what life will offer and eager with anticipation to face each day with a brand-new sense of excitement. The Gatekeeper puts themselves in the path of truth and gratitude because they know that is where the light reaches. They want to grow, so they are grateful to be planted beneath the dark spaces of the soil. They know it is not only necessary but also temporary, and that someday they will reach the light. Because of this, they do not fear darkness either.

The Gatekeeper knows that life is a cycle and so she/he keeps on with the flow, keeps on allowing, keeps on being courageous and stays open to receive.

The Creator

"Gratitude is the highest and purest demonstration of love."
~Bernice Angoh

"Feeling gratitude and not expressing it is like wrapping a present and not giving it."
~William Arthur Ward

"To speak gratitude is courteous and pleasant, to enact gratitude is generous and noble, but to live gratitude is to touch heaven."
~Johannes A. Geartner

When the Rebel, the Gatekeeper, the Healer, and the Creator collide, new worlds emerge. The creation of these new worlds is nothing but an outward mirroring of the inner world. The creator is much like the sun that gives and never asks back; like the tree that bears fruit for the eating pleasure of another; like the bee that makes honey even when its only reward is fire; like the rain that quenches and revives that which was once dry, or dead. The Creator is love. Not romantic love, which is mostly concerned with self, but love that is spoken in action and is selfless.

"Gratitude is an outward expression of appreciation; appreciation is outwardly shown through kindness; kindness is an overflow of inner love."
~Bernice Angoh

Gratitude is an awareness of self in everyone you meet and a deeper awareness that all you have is most enjoyable only when shared. It is a pilgrimage between hearts where the universe is the only audience. Let me tell you a story that clearly illustrates an attitude of gratitude:

Diana was a single mom of five children who barely made enough to keep the roof over her head or food on the table, but she never showed any signs of frustration or bitterness.

"But mother, we've barely got food to last a few days." The oldest said, watching her mother divide the groceries in three parts. She had two best friends with whom she always shared her groceries. It did not matter if she had one tomato, she would slice it into three and made sure they each had a piece.

"Go, give each of them a bag. It should hold them for a few days too." Diana would say.

The children could never understand why she insisted on doing that. They tried to reason with her, but it was futile.

"What if we run out of food?"

"You will see, my daughter, the hand that is open to give is also open to receive. Have we ever gone without?" She would ask.

"No, we haven't" her children would respond.

"Go and give these to my friends, they are hungry too, and they have children too. I cannot be happy if they have nothing to eat. Whatever I have is theirs also."

As it would happen the children never remembered a time they went without. It was like magic, that each time before food ran out, an uncle or far off relative passing through town would suddenly drop by with a trunk full of food: a bunch of plantains, rice, palm oil, eggs, and some vegetables.

"You know, I just remembered you lived in the city and decided to pay you a visit to see how things are going for you. Come, I have some gifts in the back of the car. Children, help your mother unload the trunk."

And yes, even that too she divided into three, one portion for her household and the other two portions for her two friends. But it was not only her closest friends she did this for. She was kind and giving to everyone who needed help; if she had, she gave. Even when she had a little, she gave a little out of the little.

That woman in the story is my mother, Diana.

"The fruits of gratitude are only ever felt."
-Bernice Angoh

I remember being eight years old and curious about why my mother always put food aside when she cooked. But it was not just food, she set aside toiletries and clothes. My stepdad had a respectable job at that time and our family was still intact. Anyway, one day I asked her to take me with her on one of her errands and she agreed. On reaching the location, my heart broke. It was impossible to think, that not too far from where we lived, in a beautiful five-bedroom house, our neighbor barely had a hut for a house. The zinc roof had rusted, and rain dripped through the holes from the top. The walls of the cramped space were made from mud. In that little space was an old, worn mattress, a little fire side with three stones that held a little pot and a few plastic dishes stacked against the wall. In the corner, a little baby girl cried helplessly; obviously irritated from her cold, as evidenced by her runny nose. I was in shock. I watched how the lady gently placed the baby down on the bare mattress to reach up and hug my mother very tightly. She called my mother 'maman,' French for 'Mother.' My mother had been bringing her food every day since her husband had abandoned her with the baby. Having no education or skills to seek any form of employment, she had become severely depressed and had been shunned by her family. My mother never made her feel like she was less of a person, she sat on the floor in that tiny space as comfortably as she could and played with that dirty baby as if she were hers. As we were leaving, Mother promised to return with some cold medicine for the baby. We left without me finding my voice to breathe one word that day. That was the day I learned gratitude from my mother. I learned that gratitude was a giver, a giver who is aware of how much they've been given."

I learned that the word thanksgiving, is not just to speak words, nor was it to fill our bellies while counting our blessings. Thanks-giving is the giving of self, to participate in the creation of ripples, ripples of love and kindness towards the goodwill of humankind. Love and kindness are the two most important fruits of gratitude."

Gratitude is rebellious, she has walked through the fire and embodied the Healer. The Healer who becomes the giver.

The Seven Vices Of Gratitude & How To Combat Them

1. Complaining:

Complaining sucks out all the joy in any given moment and where there is no joy, there is absolutely no room for gratitude. One sure way to catch yourself when you start complaining is to ask yourself two questions; can I change this right now and are there solutions to this? If you cannot change anything now, let it go, if you can, focus on the solutions, write them down and begin to see how to implement each one. Do not be afraid to solicit the help of close friends and/or family.

2. Worry:

Most worry is negative thinking. Worry is rigid-fun. And remember rigid-fun creates no space for possibilities, awe, and adventure. It stagnates and suffocates. It is no wonder that in old English, the word 'worry' means 'to strangle' and in Middle English, the original meaning is to 'seize by the throat and tear.' Statistically, 90% of the things we worry about never happen. So, why do we allow ourselves to be tormented by these fears and negative thoughts?

Is it because over the years we have conditioned our minds to always take this route or because it satisfies our need to be in control? The good news is that we can recondition our minds to start 'taking a different route' by choosing to not identify ourselves with these thoughts. We allow them to 'walk right by' and consciously replace them with more agreeable ones. We must accept that life is riddled with uncertainties. Let the Rebel in you attack these uncertainties with an air of possibility and impending adventure. This makes room for the Healer to envision favorable outcomes rather than suffer the self with worry.

3. Anxiety:

Anxiety and worry are very closely related. Worry begets nervousness and anxiety is just that, nervousness. To be anxious is to carry self-suffering thoughts about a particular situation. This is the source of all anguish. From the old French, the word 'Anguish' means, 'acute pain' or 'tightness.' Some ways to ease anxiety and allow room to practice gratitude is to listen to music, meditate, journal, exercise, eat a well-balanced meal and get enough sleep. If your anxiety becomes too overwhelming, seek medical help or other forms of therapy.

4. Unforgiveness:

Forgiveness, like gratitude, is a giver; giving oneself the permission to let love take the place of guilt, shame, anger, and resentment. Forgiveness is 'for giving,' not to withhold. To extend a helping hand to oneself and/or to another. The one thing forgiveness does is to open the gate to endless possibilities. Forgiveness is the Rebel handing over the keys of surrender to the Gatekeeper, and those are the keys to the healing room where all good fruits come from. Forgiveness is a surefire way to express self-love. It is impossible to express gratitude with an unforgiving heart. Its fruits are most bitter to the one withholding forgiveness. If there is any guilt, shame, resentment, or anger inside you, weed them out for they will choke the beautiful flowers trying to grow within. An awakened person knows that unforgiveness is just a slower form of suicide.

5. Selfishness:

Selfishness is the mask of a narcissist. Narcissist never can truly practice gratitude because they are takers not givers. All their contributions are towards self-satisfaction which is their highest goal. Selfishness prevents from seeing the needs of others because the self is insatiable. The room of love in a selfish person is empty. Gratitude is the purest and highest expression of love, and what you do not have you cannot give. One way to become more selfless is to cultivate the mindset of walking in others' shoes. An awakened person often goes out of your way to assist and help others in need not for recognition or a reward but as a contribution to creation.

6. Envy:

Envy is a self-loather. She says, 'Because the other person has what I want or don't have, it means either I'm not worthy or not deserving, and I'm not deserving because there's something not quite right with me." This discontentment with oneself fuels resentment. An awakened mind cannot be envious, instead it rejoices in the accomplishments and good qualities of others. There is an awareness, a shared joy in knowing that someone has gotten what they had hoped/prayed for. An awakened person knows that envy is the laziest compliment.

7. Hate:

Hate is a synonym for fear. The opposite of hate is not love; it is fear. An awakened person is one who has become fearless. Where there is fear, love has run out of oxygen. Where there is love, there will you also find gratitude.

All seven vices of gratitude include either some form of control which leads to suffering and pain; the only cure for which is to surrender. Surrender is a mighty-winged eagle.

"Gratitude can never be counted, measured or quantified; it is as immeasurable as tears, as infinite as love and as unspoken as silence, yet as loud as the heat on a hot summer's day."

-Bernice Angoh

All who practice GRATITUDE are GREAT-FULL.

IN CONCLUSION

In conclusion, there is no such thing as manifesting, nor do we need to do much for it to occur: Everything is a Happening.

Yes, in the beginning, like a young child, we may need help/support in the form of rituals, guides, books, and mentors. But as we grow and mature from spiritual infancy, we discover that what's most important is love, and love is surrender. So, when the soul comes calling, listen, then act according to the nudge or urge.

When you need nothing, it is then you've opened the flood gates for everything.

"Hari nam sat nam hari nam hari. Hari nam sat nam sat nam hari" is a Sanskrit mantra which simply means:

"Align the powerful creative flow of life with my destiny, and my intuitions with my intention, so that the unseen hand of spirit supports my fulfillment."

IMAGINE (IMAGE-IN) THIS...

In another dimension you're under a lovely lavender tree, hands underneath your head with a big smile on your face. The air smells of April showers, and a light wind flirts with your hair. It's a beautiful day to just be. So, you close your eyes and begin to reminisce about a life, this life.

Though you were there for only a few minutes, it seems you had been laying under that tree for decades. Everything you reminisced about felt real. Time slowed down for you to experience everything once more as though you were experiencing it for the very first time. You went right to the beginning when you were first born. Oh, the first heartbreak; the first kiss; the first time you betrayed someone else, etc. You relived it all.

Days passed, then months, and soon years that never seemed to end…it was all there as if it never was before, brand new. You had a different name, different face and you were engrossed in it all that you forgot to remind yourself you were under the lavender tree just reminiscing, and none of what you saw in your mind's eye was real.

All of life is just a remembering, and at this very moment I am remembering writing this book and these words to you as you are remembering reading these words in front of your eyes. They fool you, these five senses, don't they? But then, that's the only way to fully be in the moment and experience the play. Could you change something if you chose to? I'm certain you could, but you know, your HIGHER SELF knows what a masterpiece the whole story is and just wants to enjoy 'reading' and 'remembering' it just as it was written. After all, there are other versions of the story she may choose to reminisce come tomorrow. Perhaps this time she would be by a brook reminiscing about that time when she was a boy.

Maybe it's all just a memory; maybe we are all just reliving memories…in this life that we think is so real, we are all just daydreaming of a life we once experienced and marveling at how far we've come…we are the 'future' having a ball retelling all that has been… soon we will wake up and realize there was never anything we should have been afraid of and that we were just playing with shadows.

~BERNICE ANGOH

All is well and unfolding as it should. There is nothing left to do Little Dreamer. Relax into the dream.

~BERNICE ANGOH

All of life is a pregnancy, and birth awaits on the other side.

~BERNICE ANGOH

ABOUT BERNICE

Originally from Cameroon, West Africa, Bernice Angoh has an impressive body of work that spans three decades. From several nominations for 'Poet of the year' to winning Editor's choice awards on multiple occasions, her work has been published in anthologies, magazines and hailed as transformational, soul-stirring and divinely inspired. Her latest publication in *Chicken Soup for the Soul* (My (kind) America), is one of many collaborations and contributions in the literary world. "Goddess of Love," "Love Alchemist," "Rumi woman Incarnate" and "The consummate word weaver" are only a few of the titles she has garnered from readers, fans, and those who've had the opportunity to work closely with her.

As a mystic there are no topics Ms. Angoh shies away from. Her wealth of knowledge comes from a place of deep compassion, kindness, and love.

Connect with Bernice:

www.berniceangoh.com
www.paperheartbook.com
www.twinflamemanifestation.com

Tiktok handle:
@iam_magic9

Other published and upcoming titles by Ms. Angoh:

1. How to attract a specific love partner: The ONLY book you will ever need on finding your spirit-mate & exploring the joys of sacred unions.
2. Unbecoming You
3. Ananda
4. In One Breath (Volume 1-4)

Printed in Great Britain
by Amazon

16093543R00086